4 Easy Steps to Your Affiliate Marketing Success

Simple Strategies for Establishing Your Passive Income Business

JOSEPH DAVIDSON

CONTENTS

This page intentionally left blank

Introduction

Often most people come across many difficulties on their ways of affiliate business. They feel themselves weak for overcoming barriers when meet unknown issues and troubles, experience disappointed emotions and sometimes give up everything they have started. That's pity!

Though affiliate marketing isn't a rocket science and hard to do business, it also requires some particular knowledge, skills and patience for getting notable results.

When I have heard about affiliate marketing initially I was too skeptical about it. Though I was familiar with the impressive results of many affiliates, it seemed to me as a hard to do and unreachable task.

But in fact the reality was completely different. The only issue and skeptics which were preventing me to put my first steps to my passive income were only my personal negative impressions and feelings in my mind. The lack of knowledge about affiliate marketing made me fear about failures and blinded my eyes from seeing marvelous and profitable sides of it.

But fortunately, after a short time I have started to learn affiliate marketing deeper and wider. I have researched a lot by learning the ways and methods of many successful affiliates.

Days, weeks and months passed… In the end, all gathered materials: tips, recommendations, strategies, tricks, "dos and don'ts" from successful affiliates and online entrepreneurs which were written publicly or given me personally changed my mind and my business orientation. That was the power of knowledge and experience. Yes! It was the knowledge, which sorted all affiliates into *"Successful"* and *"Unsuccessful"* categories.

Several months ago without this knowledge I was standing in front of a big dilemma with these questions:

- *"What is affiliate marketing?"*
- *"How can I do it?"*
- *"Is it possible to make a living by affiliate marketing?"*

- *"May I begin it without any investment?"*
- *"What happens, if..?"*

But today all doubts and uncertain feelings are blown away from my mind.

SO, WHAT KIND OF BOOK THIS IS?

Current book can be a handbook and practical guide for affiliates, especially for new beginners, helping them to establish the right affiliate business, increase their knowledge, revenues and avoid from big mistakes.

While writing my current book I have tried to be short, concrete and honest, instead of spinning your mind with flashing, dishonest and empty notions. I hope you'll understand me at the end of the reading.

Besides, at the end of the book I've listed some top and useful websites. I believe that these recommended websites will show you the right way and make your works easier.

DEAR READER! PLEASE KEEP IN MIND, THIS IS:

- *Not a comprehensive book of affiliate marketing.*

- *Not a personal success story.*
- *Not a flashing "Trust me and make millions quickly!" deception.*
- *Not a viral product, containing affiliate links.*
- *Not a "Buy my proven money making system!" and etc.*

"4 Easy Steps to Your Affiliate Marketing Success: Simple Strategies for Establishing Your Passive Income Business" is the book of affiliate marketing strategies and methods about getting considerable results with four easy steps.

In the course of reading you will get knowledge about affiliate marketing essentials, selecting the right niche, establishing an audience and platform and using various promoting methods and others.

HOW TO GET MORE VALUE FROM THIS BOOK

First, read the whole book and try to understand the written techniques and tips.

Any simple seemed plain tip, written in the short section may be the critical part of your future affiliate business.

For example, I've seen and listened hundred times about the importance of putting the needs of an audience in the first place than thinking about how to earn more money by promoting and offering unwelcome products. Strategies like this may be written in any place of my any chapter, but some of them are really crucial and life changing. You will later know (or already have known) that many people on the Internet have written (and are writing) countless blog posts, articles, reports, even some writers have created 30-35 pages e-books about the tips that I have also explained in my book.

Most of the methods written in this book have already turned into the biggest principles of some winning and top earning affiliates. So, don't rush and be patient.

I wish you good reading and affiliate millions!

Good Luck!

This page intentionally left blank

STEP 1 – KNOW ABOUT AFFILIATE MARKETING

Definition of Affiliate Marketing

Affiliate marketing is one of the types of Internet businesses and the form of performance based marketing in which affiliates get commissions for their promoting endeavors.

There are four major participants in affiliate marketing: the merchant, the network, the affiliate and the customer.

As a merchant it may be any brand or person which sells products or services, a network gives offers for affiliates and takes care of the payments, an affiliate promotes affiliate products or services for a commission and a customer purchases the stuff promoted by affiliates.

Usually affiliates insert hosting (affiliate) links with banners and product reviews on their blogs, websites, social networks, viral products and other reachable places for the people online. When visitors click on these affiliate links and make a purchase, affiliates will get a commission from this sale. This is really what the affiliate marketing is.

Being an affiliate starts with the submission to any affiliate program or system. After being a member and getting an account, affiliates may choose a subject in the marketplace and then promote products or services by using various methods.

Benefits of Affiliate Marketing

The biggest benefit of affiliate marketing is that any person who is able to use a computer and Internet with basics is able to do it.

There are no any limitations or discriminations in this business. Any person who has the intention for making money on the Internet may turn his/her life into passive income lifestyle by applying commonly or individually used marketing techniques and strategies.

Being a successful affiliate marketer does not depend on your gender, nationality, age, education level, profession and etc. You may join any kind of affiliate network or program and earn how much you want. This sounds great! But, as I've written before there is a grand requirement for being successful in this business. I'll tell you about this later.

But, now let me tell you about some of the benefits of being an affiliate marketer.

Zero or Little Business Investment

In affiliate marketing you can start with little or without any financial investment. Most successful affiliates invest some little money for establishing their websites and blogs. But some of them even start without any money using just free promoting methods like free blogs, forums, revenue sharing websites, viral products, social media, etc. That's why affiliate marketing attracts numerous people online who are eager to start their Internet business with limited capital.

Time and Money Freedom

For succeeding in affiliate business you don't need to any employees or special working hours. Everything depends on you. The more time and effort you deposit, the more money and success you get. Because in affiliate marketing income is not limited and it is almost up to you how much to work and how much to earn. For example, once successfully created affiliate business or good written product review may turn into a passive income, which may bring capital even when you are not working.

High Diversity

Affiliate marketing can fit to almost any person and any subject you're interested in. There are various profitable subjects (niches) which you can find, promote and make nice incomes from them.

Without Expert Knowledge

It isn't necessary to be an expert in the field you are working and promoting affiliate stuffs. For example, if you are promoting skin care products, you don't need to be a dermatologist or a skin care specialist. All you have to do is advertising and marketing these affiliate products properly and professionally.

Limitless Programs

There are many affiliate programs and networks on the Internet which you can join and make excellent profits from them.

This page intentionally left blank

STEP 2 – SELECT YOUR RIGHT NICHE

Definition of Niche

"Niche" and *"Niche Marketing"* are frequently used terms in affiliate marketing.

Niche is a category or sub category that you choose in marketplace of any affiliate network. Usually these categories may be different in every affiliate system and also they are distinguished by their particularities.

Here is an example of a niche and its sub niches:

BODYBUILDING

- *Exercises*
  - o *Weigh loss exercises*
  - o *Mass gain exercises*
- *Nutrition*
  - o *Fat loss diets*
  - o *Muscle gain diets*
- *Supplements*
  - o *Fat loss supplements*
  - o *Mass gain supplements*

Importance of Choosing a Right Niche

Experts and top earning affiliates affirm that the essence of selecting a right niche is so high that it's almost impossible to get substantial results without choosing the right niche.

Here are two very considerable factors of choosing a niche:

It Helps People Quicker Find What They Search for

Most Internet users seek for something special and interesting for them. Only a small amount of people enter Internet without any clear purpose. For example, minorities of Internet users' type in search engines as *"food"*, but majorities of them write as *"healthy food recipes"*, *"weigh loss food recipes"*, *"recipes for beautiful skin"*, etc. It means that if your website is not relevant to what people search for they will exit and go to somewhere else which is more relevant for their purpose.

It Increases Your Search Engine Ranking

If your website is too general, then the chances of getting high traffic will be so low. Search engines can't send you traffic if they don't know what your website is really about. Imagine your website is about *"Health and Beauty"* and people are seeking for *"Melanoma"*. In this case can you guarantee them to find the exact answer they are seeking for? Will search engines send these people who are interested in this type of skin cancer to the website which is just about health and beauty? The answer is *"No"*, of course. In this situation websites which are related to skin cancer problems will be more helpful.

Except these reasons, selecting a right niche helps you to avoid from various traumatic situations and serves to prevent upcoming failures on the way of your affiliate business.

Strategies for Choosing a Proper Niche

For finding the right niche you must know the exact answers for these three questions:

What are Your Interests or What You Love to Do?

It is clear to everybody that living and working with interests make people happier and their life easier. One of the benefits of doing what you love is that you may not often feel many tedious difficulties which occur on your way. You take pleasure and work with enthusiasm by doing the job which you are passionate about. Therefore, choose a subject you are really fervent about.

Are You Good at the Subject You Have Opted?

You should always be aware of what you are promoting. Most successful affiliates say that it is impossible and prosperity is not guaranteed if you are trying to move your affiliate business with not knowing the products you are promoting. *How would you recommend something to people if you don't know it?* I think it's dishonest and impossible. If possible, it will be short life opportunity. So, recommend and promote products or services which you have tested before.

Do People Spend Money in the Subject You Have Chosen?

There are limitless high demand products and services on the Internet which people are seeking every day. But on the other hand, these products and services will also be high competing and hard to win among other high skilled and experienced affiliates. But even so, it is also possible for you to endeavor and attain some substantial results almost in every market.

When you choose a subject for beginning don't just dive into the categories in the market. Do some research, don't go too broad and narrow your selection. For example, choose *"Health and Fitness"* category, narrow it to the subject *"Exercises"* and then you may narrow it again to *"Fat loss exercises"* and so on. This is really productive and helps you to avoid from high competition.

But the biggest *"You must do!"* here is supplying your audience with what they actually need. Here are strategies:

Think! What Do People Really Seek and Need for?

People on the Internet always search for something special. It may be an answer for their request, a solution for their problem or just any appealing information. Always know about the needs of your audience.

Think! Which Products or Services Do Actually Solve People's Problems?

This must be your daily using principle or slogan of your affiliate business. If you promote helpless or unwanted products and services (even if you use the greatest methods and techniques) people will not buy them. And the worst of all, later you may lose your all gathered reputation and credibility.

Think! What Makes People Completely Satisfied and Happy?

The only thing that makes customers pleased and happy is high quality and helpful products. They'll be delighted only when they get expected positive results with their purchase.

This page intentionally left blank

STEP 3 – BE FAMILIAR WITH YOUR AUDIENCE

Significance of Knowing Audience

Audience is a visitor, reader or listener in your platform. As an audience there may be any kind of person. For example, an athlete, a student, a gardener, a physicist, an entrepreneur, etc.

In audience interests and intentions will be various and special for each of people coming from their needs. For example, an athlete may be eager to develop his/her athletic skills; a student would like to obtain any foreign language study guide; a hair stylist tries to be aware of the latest hair styling techniques and so on.

It is well known that in any kind of online or offline business finding a target audience is very important. If your audience likes your products or services, your commerce will grow. If not, your business will break down very soon.

In affiliate marketing being familiar with your target audience is second vital step after choosing a niche. First, you have to identify the people behind your niche and then provide them with what they actually need or want. Solving the problems of your audience and satisfying them with your works is the biggest principle of affiliate marketing. If you do it right, believe me, very soon you will be the next high earning affiliate marketer.

So, how can you identify your target audience?

Read the next section!

Questions for Determining Your Audience

If you want to know your audience, just answer to these simple questions.

Who are the visitors in your platform?

Who are your viewers or listeners?

For whom are you going to offer your products or services?

Let's learn an example.

Imagine you have a website about natural bodybuilding. In this platform you offer people various products, free workout programs, articles about nutrition and supplements, motivational sections and so forth.

In this website your target audience will be the people who are interested in natural bodybuilding. They may be professionals or amateurs, teenagers or adults and any other people who are passionate about natural bodybuilding.

After that you may find appropriate answers for these questions too:

What do they like and dislike?

What does motivate them?

What kind of products and characters do they like?

Which keywords do they use?

Why are they coming to you or what is attracting them?

Make a little research and find at least 5 answers for each above written inquires.

This page intentionally left blank

STEP 4 – CHOOSE PRODUCTIVE WAYS OF PROMOTING

After choosing your affiliate stuff, you will necessarily need to promote them with any method. Here we learn some of the biggest and most effective ways of promoting.

Websites and Blogs: How to Create and Optimize Them Properly

Without any doubt, applying your personal website as a primary promoting method is the biggest, the most effective and the easiest way of succeeding in affiliate business.

In your website you can control almost every effort you do: centralize, gather all your created ads and proceedings, link other promoting methods with each other, etc. This is definitely easy manageable and comfortable for controlling your affiliate business.

Have you ever seen any successful affiliate marketer who doesn't have his/her personal website or blog? I think you have never seen that. It's almost impossible to get normal results in affiliate marketing without having a website or blog. If so, your number one priority should be creating a personal website or blog.

There are two options for getting a website: *Buying a ready one* or *Building it personally.* Both of them have advantages and disadvantages.

If you absolutely don't know how to create a website and intend to buy a ready one, search for it on the Internet. There are numerous profitable and ready offers by website creators and owners.

But most affiliates prefer to creating their own website rather than just buying a ready one.

Website creating and developing take not only more time and effort, but also require some knowledge, skills and patience.

Generally, a winning and an expedient website should be:

- *Simple*
- *Well designed*
- *Well arranged*
- *Easy to review*
- *Informative*
- *Inspiring*
- *Helpful.*

When most people use Internet or enter any website they commonly search for a solution for their problems. They always will be oriented to any direction. For example, a foreign bachelor's degree graduating student may seek for any master degree program, a bodybuilding amateur might search for any mass gaining supplements, a fantastic genre book reader could look for any new published e-books, etc.

Every single day millions of Internet users around the world enter the net with any special purpose. But, while searching on the Internet they usually feel these psychological feelings:

- *Need.* As I said before majority of Internet users don't just enter websites without any clear purpose. They will always be strongly oriented with certain needs and requires.

- *Pain.* Every person in the world feels this physical and psychological feeling. Living without it is absolutely impossible and unavoidable. It doesn't matter what you offer them and how great your proposal seems; believe me, if you find a solution to their problems and suffers, they will also give you real value as a replacement for it.

- *Fear.* As fear it may be the fear of spending or losing money on the product they are going to buy, the fear of getting negative results by using it, etc. In this case you have to provide them with trust, veracity and other helpful comprehensions to break their fear and anxiety.

- *Skeptics.* As some experts say only about two or three visitors out of hundred (or hundreds) may buy the stuff you are offering in your website. Others would be too skeptical and often leave your website with just a click of their mouse. So, if you wish hundreds of people buy your product, you have to make thousands or millions of them enter your web page.

So, what do you need for creating a website?

Website building is not a rocket science, but, as I said before it takes time, little capital and endurance to be successful. For beginning you should know about how to get a domain name, web hosting, theme creating, mailing services, SEO (Search Engine Optimization), content writing, using necessary keywords, organizing website layout and many others. After getting this basic knowledge about website establishing it will be easier to run your business even if you employ any specialist or use any certain service.

Let's start learning them!

Choosing a Domain Name

Selecting a good domain name is an essential part of website creating. As your online identity, it says a lot about you or your running industry.

Domain name is a part of network address that identifies it as belonging to a particular field. For example: *nytimes.com, harvard.edu, wikipedia.org, spain.info, sourceforge.net*, etc.

Follow these tips for creating a successful domain name:

Select a Name Relevant to the Field You Choose

The domain name of your website should reveal its main function and provide your readers with the first impression about your website occupation. When people see your domain name for the first time, they should promptly imagine what kind of content they may find in your website.

You may use your primary keyword or brand name as your domain name. For example, when we see *www.bodybuilding.com* we instantly recognize that website is about bodybuilding, *www.apple.com* is a domain taken from a brand name, etc.

Keep It Short and Simple

Usually short names are easy to type and easier to remember. Simplicity and brevity is the best strategy in this case.

Make It Easy to Remember

If you select difficult and hard to keep in mind domain names, it will be complicated for site reviewers to recall it. That's why just give simple and easy to remember names for your domain.

Choose a Catchy Name

Almost in every business choosing an attractive name plays a significant role for winning in this matter. Don't be unconcerned to this reality.

Don't Use Numbers and Hyphens

They may be confusing, hard for typing and not easy to remember. Often winning domain names don't contain numbers and hyphens.

Use Popular Domain Extensions

.COM, .ORG, .NET, .INFO are still most popular and preferable domain names to use.

Using a Hosting Service

What is web hosting?

Web hosting is one of the crucial steps of website building. It is a service which provides space for users to store their website content. Website information such as images, videos, or any other content accessible through the web needs to be stored on a computer server located in a secure and climate controlled environment which is permanently connected to the Internet through high speed data lines. This server space is called as web hosting.

There are numerous and various web hosting companies and services on the Internet. They differ from each other by their prices, services and qualities.

Often finding an optimal and appropriate hosting service may be an overwhelming process, especially for new website creators.

Here are some tips for choosing a good hosting service:

Don't Chase Free Web Hostings

Although free service sounds good, later it may not be so effective as it has seemed before. If you wish to earn money by using your website, you have to find reliable and assured services which can take responsibilities by their side. Usually any kind of good quality hosting services cost some money. For this reason don't afraid of wasting some extra money for high value hosting packages.

Choose a Host, Not a Price

Price is not a sign of web host quality. Take a little bit time and make a research about what kind of services they offer.

Try Short Term Contracts Before

Like most other services web hosting also offers some discounts for long term contracts and asks for payments in advance for multi month or yearly contracts. I strongly recommend to try out a new hosting service for one or two months and also ensure the contract termination and money back policies before.

Separately Register Your Domain Name

If something goes wrong with your web host, there will not be a chance to detain your domain name too. So, register your domain and hosting individually.

Efficient Customer Support

Usually admirable customer services may save your time and prevent some future frustrations. Connect with a customer support team for solving any issue that you have and check its quality and efficiency before making any decisions. It should be easy to get in touch with them and they should help you in a nice and professional way.

Find a Hosting Service that Proclaims Down Times

Usually web hosts frequently update their servers and in this case your website will also be unavailable when this process happens. Therefore, select a service that tells you in advance when your site will be down. Updating procedure should be when you are not getting lots of visits.

Pick a Company that Offers You Detailed Site Statistics

It is better to choose a hosting service which suggests statistics and traffic info to your website.

Choose Secure Payment Methods

Make sure that hosting service accepts well-known and secure payment methods too.

Establishing a Website

As statistics shows most people don't read online while surfing on web pages, they just scan. They stop scanning whenever something catches their attention. When something captures their interest, then they will read it deeper and in details. This is very considerable factor in website building and designing. If you create and design your website properly and professionally this will bring you high amount of traffic.

Designing websites and web pages demand some knowledge, skills, tricks and abilities. If you are new beginner and not able to do it for yourself, recruit a professional web designer.

While establishing your website or webpage you should seriously pay attention to its layout.

Website layout is a setting of different elements which creates a website. This includes creating a webpage structure; choosing a theme, color, fonts, graphics and logo; inserting multimedia files; setting menu and navigation buttons; linking ads; mailing and many others.

Search on the Internet for *"website layout tips and tricks"* and make a little research about them. Dedicate your two or three hours for studying website layout building and designing techniques. But, as I said before recruiting a professional and honest specialist is the best way to do it for "thumb".

Writing Content

Creating a well organized, concise and attractive content is a vital part of website building. You can't get a perfect website with poorly written content. Therefore, there is a famous slogan: *"Content is the King"*.

Though many website owners write their content personally, others prefer to recruit professional content writers.

There are two types of content: *Story type* and *Editorial type*.

Story Type of Content

In this type of content you can write a short story about how you have (or someone has) achieved something by using the product or service you are promoting. Here you should illustrate to your audience how the person you are telling about was similar to them and then got positive results by using the product or service you are offering them as well.

Typically, people online search for the solution to their problems and perhaps that's why they have found you. Imagine, what happens in a reader's mind when he/she finds a similar story which has been changed one's life into the marvelous side that he/she also wanted to reach. Therefore most content writers often use their inspiring personal success stories to encourage their readers for getting the exact positive results as they have got in the past.

Editorial Type of Content

In this type of content you have to write a professional article about the product you are promoting or offering to your audience.

Here are some tips which may help you for creating a successful content:

Use Bulleted Lists to Express Your Ideas

When you are writing about something you may list its advantages and disadvantages, its specifics, its benefits and others by using bulleted lists. This method helps your website visitors to understand you better, easier and faster.

Use Bold, Italic, Underlined and Uppercase Writing Techniques

If you want your keywords or terms to be seen easily, just use these above mentioned techniques to emphasize them. Without any doubt, highlighted words or sentences will be displayed initially to the eyes of readers than the ones that are not distinguished.

Don't Create Long Paragraphs

As statistics shows people online usually tend to read short sections than long ones. If they are prolonged and tedious, they will jump from long paragraphs to shorter ones or even leave the webpage. Make your paragraphs easy reading, short and concise.

Create a Catchy Title

Well selected name or title is half success in any business. The chosen title should reveal the main meaning of the subject you are writing and totally explain what the issue is about.

Be Objective

Avoid from flashing and boasting *"This is the best..."*, *"This is complete and perfect..."* claims. Instead of them let people come to that conclusion on their own.

Use a Reversed Pyramid Method of Writing

Write your main ideas, points and conclusion on the first place of the text. Most web readers are impatient and don't want to read the topic until the end.

Use Right Keywords

Appropriate keywords in content writing are special words which people use while searching on the Internet. Apply at least 100-300 important keywords in your content and arrange them at the beginning and also at the end of your content. Make sure that you have not overused keywords, but you have spread them over your content wisely and normally.

Write an Original Content

Plagiarism will be punished by search engines. So, make a little research and create your own content.

Insert Pictures or Videos

Adding eye-catching and cute images related to your content will capture the attention of your website visitors and makes them glance for a moment. Make your well written plain text interesting with appealing images.

Check Spelling and Grammar

Spelling and grammar mistakes make people stop reading your content and jump from your website to another one. Proofread your content several times before embedding it into your webpage.

SEO (Search Engine Optimization)

Search engine optimization is an aggregate of various optimizing strategies and techniques used to boost the ranking of a website in search engine results page like Google, Yahoo, Bing, etc.

Usually website owners try to improve their website ranking in search results by optimizing its content and structure. They want it to be recognized by search engines.

Generally SEO reveals the secrets of how search engines work, what people search for and which keywords they use and many others.

If you have a website and want it to be seen on the top page of search results, you will need to know about the nuances of SEO. Surely, without knowing and using SEO techniques all your other efforts on website building will be worthless. If so, don't be unconcerned about Search Engine Optimization.

There are hundreds of SEO tips, tricks and strategies.

Here are some crucial ones:

Write a Unique Content

Don't copy the content of others. Search engines punish your website if you have copied someone else's content. Make a little research and create your personal and original content

Use Proper Keywords

Use appropriate keywords and phrases in your content, text body, titles, headlines, domain, URLs, etc. Pay attention to the density of your keywords and don't repeat them too much.

Make Links

Set up relevant links with other top ranked websites and social networks. Make sure that these links also connect your each webpage with each other.

Apply Sitemaps

Sitemap is a tool for easy navigation across the website. This helps web users promptly and efficiently search every page of the website.

Optimize Website

Usually long time loading of the webpage makes site visitors disappointed and not wait until its opening. It is better not to increase 100k page size and decrease unnecessary characters from webpages.

Set Up Social Networks

Create and share your posts and articles in social media like Facebook, Twitter, YouTube, etc. Ensure inserting your domain name and other relevant links there.

Hire a SEO Specialist

If you seriously want your website to be seen on the top page of search results, hire a professional. Choose an honest expert and let him/her do his/her job. Don't forget! The higher your website rank in search results, the more visitors and traffic it will receive.

Blogs

Blog is a form of website which is generally arranged in chronological order from the most recent posts to the older ones towards the bottom just like a diary or journal.

As a personal online publishing method it lets individuals simply and quickly write, publish and distribute almost everything on any matter via Internet.

As websites, blogs also include text entries, graphics, videos, comments and links with other websites.

Often most affiliate marketers use blogs within their websites and also separately from it. There are thousands of affiliates who are using web blogs as their promotional, communicative and informative target.

There are some big and crucial advantages of using blogs for affiliate marketers:

- Starting a blog is easier and quicker than starting a website;
- Mostly it doesn't cost anything to start;

- Huge opportunity of reaching hundreds or thousands of people in a day;
- An effective way of promoting affiliate products or services;
- A chance for building credibility and positioning yourself as an expert in the field you have chosen.

It is clear that blog creating doesn't require lots of knowledge and skills like website building. Therefore, today on the Internet exist more than 100 million blogs which most of them are created by ordinary people like you and me.

There are some very popular and trusted blog creating websites like www.blogger.com and www.wordpress.com which may be very easy and quick to launch even for newbie affiliate marketers.

But before starting to blog I have decided to provide you with some useful tips and tricks for preventing some future troubles which may occur on your way.

Here they are:

Identify your goals

For preventing future troubles make your long term plans before choosing free or fee-based blogging services.

Target your audience

Create a blog for them with a content that they are looking for. Everything you do should be valuable for your audience.

Write a good content

Creating high quality content is a vital part of blogging. Recruit your all best possibilities and techniques for writing a genius and moving content.

Build credibility

Appear as an expert and trusted person in the eyes of your visitors. Usually people estimate you with the result of the assist you have given to them. Always remember the golden principle of a successful affiliate marketer: *"First help, then offer".*

Don't be a "promotion person"

Putting *"subscribe"* or *"click here to buy"* links or buttons all over the pages makes your visitors displeased and annoyed. Try to be modest and helpful until people trust you and like your blog more.

Make your blog simple

Create an attractive, easy to navigate and simple blog. Simplicity is enough in blog creating.

Use a clean and simple theme

Don't apply heavy and tiresome themes. Give pleasant and inspiring mood to your audience with your cute theme.

Recruit a freelancer

If you have possibility, use a freelance service for developing your blog. An additional smart head will definitely help you solve your extra issues.

Post regularly

This is a simple and an effective way for adding more traffic to your website or blog. As an active blogger write helpful posts daily and consistently. Try to create at least one blog post everyday for getting good results and also avoid from writing long and complex ones.

Revenue Sharing Websites

Revenue sharing websites are free website platforms which allow users to create free web pages on the subjects that they are passionate about or interested in. The biggest uniqueness of these platforms is that they don't demand from users being aware of website creating and designing skills. They allow users to build pages on various topics, insert ads, reviews, content and others without having to write any HTML.

Commonly, the purpose of creating such free web pages may be different. Some of the users establish these pages just for passion, others for promoting or selling affiliate or any other stuffs.

Today such kind website creators as Squidoo, Hubpages, Bukisa, InfoBarrel, Xomba, Ukritic and others have been already popular on the Internet. Especially, most affiliates who don't have their own website or blog will be eager to use them as a promoting method.

In some cases affiliates can use these revenue sharing websites effectively. They can turn them into link building, traffic generating and referral tools.

Every revenue sharing website has its own pros and cons. The strategy, recommended for one affiliate marketer may not work for another one. Therefore, I recommend you to learn and try them personally.

Social Networks: the Compulsory Tool of Internet Marketing

Today it's clear for every Internet user that social media widely opened the doors of various, comfortable and easy communication opportunities via online.

Nowadays even people who rarely use Internet are familiar with the power and opportunities of social networks like Facebook, Twitter Google+, YouTube, Pinterest, etc.

In our days people are not only using social media as a popular method of communication, but also utilizing it as a powerful and indispensable marketing tool which brings various positive results almost in every business.

So, what is Social Media Marketing?

Social media marketing is one of the types of Internet marketing which serves to realize various marketing communications through social media networks.

By interacting and sharing different content, information, news, links, resources via social networks individuals or companies may establish easy relationship between each other and reach their valuable business goals.

Benefits of Social Media Marketing in Affiliate Business

Today it is well known for almost every affiliate marketer that applying social media networks as a communicating and marketing tool is vitally important, irreplaceable and winning strategy for running successful affiliate businesses.

It has many and particular advantages for affiliates to market their business. Here are some of them:

- Social media gives you chances to generate more links to your website;
- Using it properly brings massive traffic to your website and boosts your SEO;
- Social media facilitates you to get a larger audience;
- It costs you almost nothing to establish this word of mouth advertising, etc.

Here are some social media tips for affiliate marketing:

Don't Just Promote

Social media is created for communication, not for advertising something online. Imagine if you like or follow people in social networks and they only send you advertising links, will you then stop following them? Will it be unpleasant for you to get such promoting links? Of course "Yes". Try to set up a valuable interaction between you and others. As attending in online forums, being a "valuable person" in social media is also very important.

Use All Possible Social Media Platforms

Don't just use most famous social media like Facebook, Twitter or Google+. If you have created a website make sure that you have established several different social media networks.

Interact Productively

Try to communicate with your customers regularly. Make discussions about the topics related to the products or services you are presenting.

Viral Products: Hidden Tricks behind Them

Viral product is a digital product which is intended to spread very quickly to a large number of people. This can be a short twenty or thirty pages e-book, a 200 or 300 words containing article or special report, an amateur made video, etc.

Using viral products in affiliate marketing is an efficient and free method without ever having a website.

If you want to use viral products in affiliate marketing, create an article, e-book or video on a particular subject, insert affiliate links into there and distribute it through whatever you like. You may distribute your viral products to people for giving it away or selling. Also you may submit them on hundreds of article directories and get them published on most websites over the Internet.

Article Writing

Writing articles or promoting affiliate stuffs by using this free method is not as hard as it seems to most people. Today on the Internet thousands of online marketers are using their articles as a fast and easy success getting technique. Because it is one of the most helpful ways of advertising and selling affiliate stuffs.

Here are some major tips about article writing:

Write Only High Value Articles

As bestseller books, online articles also should be high quality, helpful, problem solving, interesting, etc. If you aim your article to be read more, learn before how to find solutions for the problems of your readers.

Use Keywords Properly

You should apply exact keywords about the subject and distribute them throughout the article with an average density. But if you overuse keywords, search engines will mark your article as a spam and make it not appear in search engine results.

Optimal Length

The length of an article should be 350-1,400 words. Don't write a long reading and boring articles.

Choose a Catchy Title

When a person views the heading of a written article he or she will be too skeptical to read it entirely. Therefore, choose an attractive and attention grabbing title for your articles.

Use Article Directory Websites

Article directory websites are those which contain list of articles of different topics. They allow you to register for an account, submit your article and publish it in their website for free.

Review the Policies of Each Website You Join

Some article directory websites may limit the amount of affiliate links you can place into each article.

Bring more Traffic

Use keyword determiner tools wisely and make your article "Search Engine Optimized" for appearing it on the top page of search results.

Book Writing

If you are able to write books, this may be a great way for you to promote your affiliate products even without having your own website or web blog.

Just write an e-book related to the subject you are promoting, insert affiliates links and submit it anywhere you want for publishing and selling. If the readers like your book, then they may visit merchant's website and make a purchase. This is much more like article writing process, but unlike article writing you can also publish, sell your books separately and make a good profit from it.

Publishing and distributing a book doesn't demand a great power and knowledge. If the book is written professionally, honestly and really helps people to solve their problems, believe me you will definitely get huge successes by publishing, distributing and selling it.

If your book is related to the affiliate issue and ready for being distributed online use book publishers for handing it out. There are hundreds of book directories on the Internet which range by their service qualities and prices. Some of them are fee-based services and others may be absolutely for free. Rules and the process of publishing books are explained in every directory and you may be familiar with them by entering these websites and reviewing their policies.

Online Discussion Communities: More than just a Communication

Online discussion community is a virtual community where people interact with each other by posting their opinions, messages, information, etc.

As online discussion communities there may be chat rooms, discussion boards, blogs, forums, social networks, etc.

Attending in online communities may be a good and productive way of being acknowledged as an expert in your chosen affiliate field.

Below I have listed several key points of using a forum as a promoting method in affiliate marketing:

Join with Top Ranked Forums

Choose and register on the forums where high amount of people are concerned and make sure that there is high traffic pending it.

Discussion Boards should be related to the Product You are Promoting

Just search on the Internet by using keywords such as *"forum"* or *"discussion board"* with the affiliate subject you are promoting. For example, if you are promoting skin care products, search for *"skin care products forum"*.

Participate Actively

This may help you to boost your affiliate income when members see you as an active and trusted person. Provide requests with the answers that are really helpful and problem solving for people. If people find you as a person who solves their issues they will also be eager to click the link you have provided in your signature box or just attempt to connect with you. Try to be an authority in the subject you discuss.

Review Member Policies

Some online communities may prohibit affiliate links and consider them as an advertising spam.

Don't Directly Insert Affiliate Links in Your Posts

Forum members dislike people who usually just write something with flashing affiliates links. Don't be this person. At the end of your post there is a signature box where you can put a promotional text and also affiliate links. This signature box will be displayed each time you reply to or write your posts.

This page intentionally left blank

MISTAKES YOU SHOULD AVOID

In any business there may be errors nearby success and victories. In affiliate business smart affiliates usually try to avoid from common mistakes which may bring great troubles.

Here are some serious mistakes that you should always be far from them.

Not Selecting a Niche

If you try to choose affiliate stuffs without opting your own niche and promote *"everything under the Sun"*, believe me, sooner or later affiliate marketing will be fully disappointed and unsuccessful for you. If you choose a wrong niche, your business will not grow and very soon you will meet with setbacks and adversities which can knock you out of the way.

Grasping too Much

If you are trying to choose as many niches as you see and promote *"everything under the Sun"* or attempting to do everything in everywhere, believe me stressful and unsuccessful days are coming to you. As I said before affiliate marketing is not about promoting everything to everybody when you meet them on your way.

Choosing Low Quality Products

Do you want to buy a low quality product for yourself? The answer is *"No"*. Of course you want to be completely satisfied with the product you have acquired. So do others. Usually people will be more skeptical, cautious and eager to quit when they are going to pay money for something unknown. You may guess results and experience feelings when an unknown person is proposing you a low quality product.

Choosing too Competitive Products

If there is high demand for a product, there will be also high competition. This may be difficult for you to succeed among other high skilled and qualified affiliates. If you are new in affiliate business, it's better to be little bit modest and get some knowledge and experience first. Don't rush!

It takes time and effort to be successful in affiliate business.

Choosing a Product that You Don't Know

It's hard and sometimes impossible to promote products that you are not familiar with. Being aware of and then recommending it to someone is usually easier to sell. So, don't attempt to promote products which you haven't verified and unknown for you.

This page intentionally left blank

Conclusion

Gradually finishing my book I've decided to write about some very important tips and key points of affiliate marketing success. If you want to be a successful affiliate marketer, don't be inattentive to these tips.

Helpfulness

Almost in every case people hesitate about the value of the products or services which they are going to purchase. If the output seems worthless they will surely decide not to deal with it.

So, make sure that your being proposed products or services are really problem solving and helpful.

Replace yourself with a potential customer and ask this question from yourself *"Would you buy it if you were in the place of the customer?"* If the answer is *"Yes"*, then the product you are promoting is really helpful and high quality. If the answer is *"No"*, then the product you are promoting is surely not helpful and low quality.

Teaching

If you are promoting any product or service, it will be your duty as an affiliate to provide your audience with the full information and knowledge about it. Reveal the features and benefits, answer the FAQ, create a video about *"How it works"* and do all your best to make people feel themselves more informed about the product or service that they are interested in.

Honesty

Affiliate marketing is all about trust. If you want to be successful in this business choose and promote only products that you also believe in. Just help people with your products or services and think only about how to solve their problems. Removing severity from their shoulders and making them happy brings you real value and more capital.

Patience

Affiliate marketing is not a get rich quick business. Succeeding in this field and seeing good results may take a little (or more) time. Don't give up if you can't see instant results and profits.

Activism

Be always active and don't wait people someday come to you. You have to be proactive by using techniques like link building, SEO and social media marketing if you want to get your website noticed and get people click on your affiliate links.

Focusing

Don't immediately choose promoting many different affiliate products on the same website. Most successful affiliates recommend promoting each unique product on a different website.

Make sure that you have focused on and provided your customers with enough information about the product you are promoting.

Knowledge

Always be eager to getting new comprehensions about affiliate marketing. Seek for new success tips, strategies, tricks, etc. Being successful demands well planned actions and smart decisions. Also learn how other affiliates have been successful in their business and what kind of mistakes they have done.

Freebies

Good marketers always use the marvelous possibilities of various discounts, freebies and gifts. Without any doubt these marketing strategies invoke good impressions in the mind of people. Don't tire of proposing free offers to the people who are interested in your products or services.

Relationship

Keep always good relationships with the people you are dealing with. This may be your website members, customers, other friendly affiliates or just any people who are interested in your activity.

You may learn too much value from the practice of honest and experienced affiliates.

Tracking

Tracking your campaigns makes your work easier and helps you to control your activities. For example, in ClickBank you can write a name or memo note on the *"ID field"*. Though it's an optional, this may be a key factor. Because this technique helps you to know about the process: who is buying your which product. Analyzing your individual campaigns is critical for determining whether you're on the right path or you need to make any changes in your strategy.

And always remember! Whatever you do any business online or offline be helpful and frank to the people you are dealing with. When you give them what they really need, sooner or later you will get a real value instead of your efforts.

Good luck!

RECOMMENDED WEBSITES

Tops Affiliate Networks for Joining:

- *www.amazon.com*
- *www.clickbank.com*
- *www.cj.com*
- *www.linkshare.com*
- *www.paydotcom.com*

Audience Defining:

- www.quantacast.com
- www.google.com/adplanner

Domain Registrars:

- www.godaddy.com
- www.webweaverelite.com
- www.namecheap.com
- www.register.com
- www.networksolutions.com

Web Hosting:

- www.hostgater.com

- www.bluehost.com

- www.web.com

- www.justhost.com

- www.ipage.com

Theme Creating:

- www.wordpress.com

- www.elegantthemes.com

- www.woothemes.com

- www.studipress.com

- www.themeforestcom

Mailing Providers:

- www.aweber.com

- www.getresponse.com

- www.icontact.com

Campaign Tracking:

- www.prosper202.com

- www.alexa.com

Keyword Tools:

- www.googlekeywordtool.com
- www.adwods.google.com
- www.seoquake.com
- www.keywordelite.com

Website Tools Creators:

- www.veripurchase.com
- www.mcafee.com
- www.hirewriters.com
- www.easywebinarplugin.com
- www.webceo.com

Search Engine Optimization (SEO):

- www.searchenginesubmitter.com

Blog Creators:

- www.blogger.com
- www.wordpress.com

Revenue Sharing Websites:

- www.squidoo.com

- www.hubpages.com

- www.bukisa.com

- www.infobarrel.com

- www.xomba.com

- www.ukritic.com

Article Writing:

- www.goarticles.com

- www.articlemarketer.com

- www.ezinearticles.com

- www.articlesbase.com

- www.articlecity.com

- www.isnare.com

- www.topezineads.com

- www.directoryofezines.com

Book Writing:

- www.book-marketing-revealed.com

- www.ebookdirectory.com

- www.wisdomebooks.com

- www.elibrary.com

Forums:

- www.big-boards.com
- www.forums.digitalpoint.com
- www.warriorforum.com

Niche Finding:

- www.nichebotclassic.com